PIANO QUARTETS
NOS. 1 AND 2

and

PIANO QUINTET
NO. 1

Gabriel Fauré

DOVER PUBLICATIONS, INC.
New York

Bibliographical Note

This Dover edition, first published in 1995, is a new compilation of three scores originally published separately. J. Hamelle, Editeur, Paris, originally published Gabriel Fauré's *1er Quatuor en ut Mineur pour Piano, Violon, Alto et Violoncelle, Op. 15,* n.d., and *2me Quatuor en Sol mineur, Op. 45,* n.d., for the same ensemble. G. Schirmer, Inc., New York, originally published Fauré's *Piano Quintet in D minor / Quintette en Ré mineur Pour Piano, Deux Violons, Alto et Violoncelle, Op. 89,* 1907.

The Dover edition adds a list of contents and two editorial notes, and makes minor corrections and clarifications in the scores.

Library of Congress Cataloging-in-Publication Data

Fauré, Gabriel, 1845–1924.
 [Chamber music. Selections]
 Piano quartets nos. 1 and 2 ; and, Piano quintet no. 1 / Gabriel Fauré.
 score. cm.
 1st and 2nd works for piano, violin, viola, and violoncello; 3rd work for piano, 2 violins, viola, and violoncello.
 Reprint (1st–2nd works). Originally published: Paris : J. Hamelle, n.d.
 Reprint (3rd work). Originally published: New York : G. Schirmer, 1907.
 ISBN 0-486-28606-1
 1. Piano quartets—Scores. 2. Piano quintets—Scores.
M178.F38C5 1995   95-12087
                                                                          CIP
                                                                           M

Manufactured in the United States of America
Dover Publications, Inc., 31 East 2nd Street, Mineola, N.Y. 11501

CONTENTS

*To Monsieur H. Léonard**

Piano Quartet No. 1 in C Minor
Op. 15
(1876–9; finale revised 1883)

*Hubert Léonard, Belgian violinist, composer and teacher, who ardently
championed the chamber music of Saint-Saëns, Fauré, Lalo and d'Indy.

I.

14 *Piano Quartet No. 1* (I)

II.

SCHERZO.

Allegro vivo. ♩. = 160.

25

III.

IV.

To Hans von Bülow

Piano Quartet No. 2 in G Minor
Op. 45 (ca. 1885–6)

I.

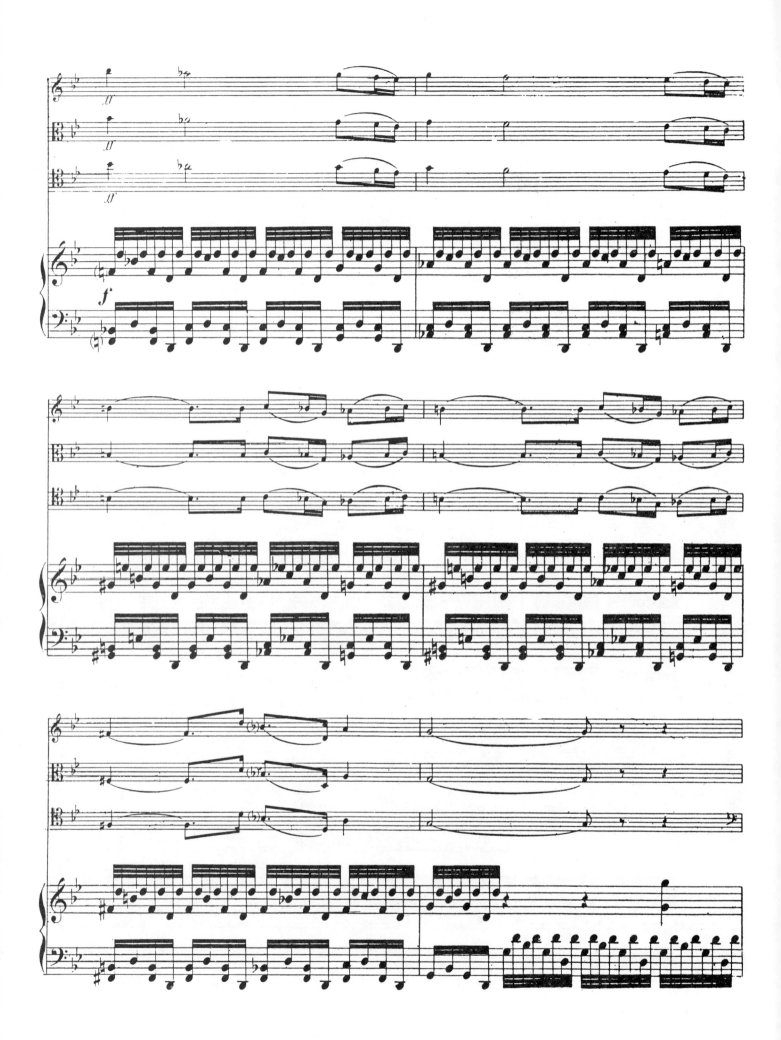

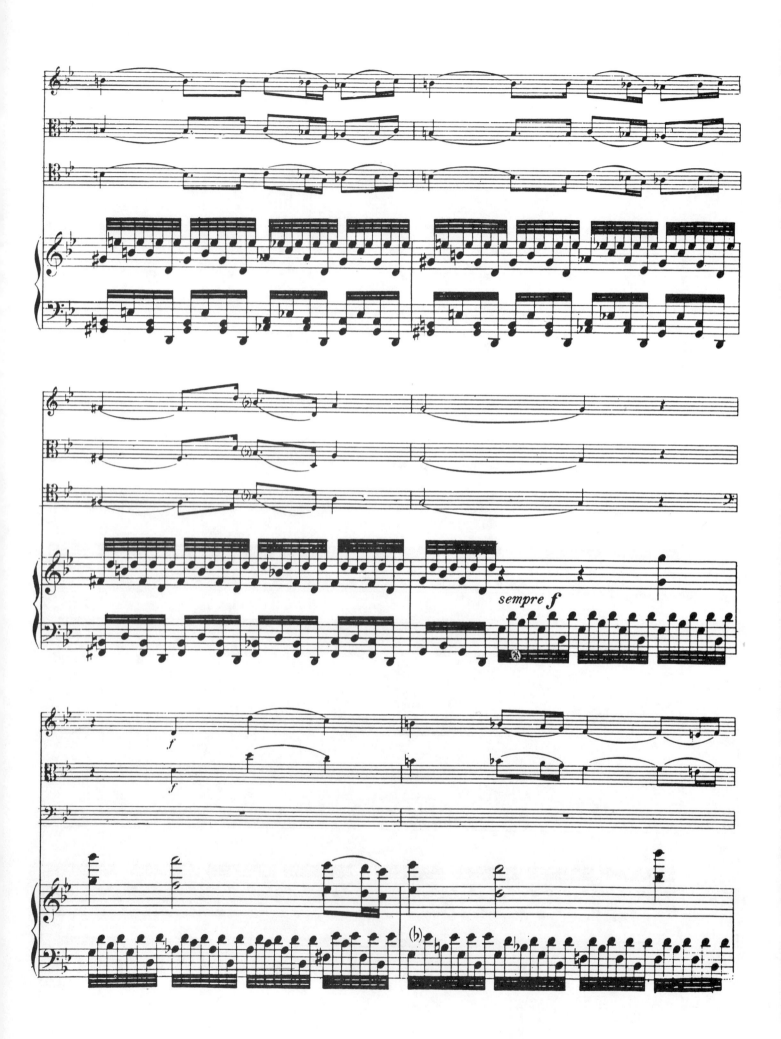

II.

III.

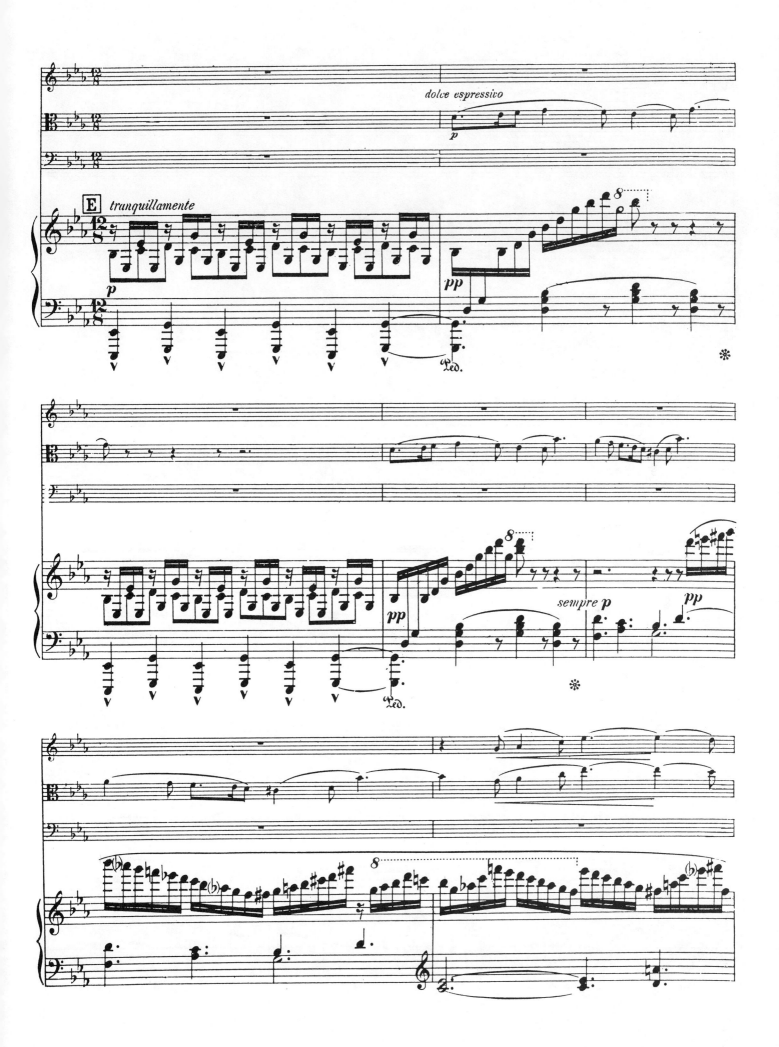

146   *Piano Quartet No. 2* (III)

IV.

164　*Piano Quartet No. 2* (IV)

To Monsieur Eugène Ysaÿe

Piano Quintet No. 1 in D Minor
Op. 89 (before 1906*)

*In Charles Koechlin's *Gabriel Fauré* (Dennis Dobson Limited, London, 1946, 2nd ed.; translated from the French by Leslie Orrey), the author speculates: "It is quite likely that the Quintet promised as Op. 60, but which never appeared (that is to say, between the *Mélodies de Venise*, Op. 58 [1891], and *la Bonne Chanson*, Op. 61 [1892–4], is none other than this Quintet . . ." For *Piano Quintet No. 1*, *Grove* gives the dates of composition as 1887–95, 1903–5. Other sources give the date 1906.

I.

II.

III.

246   *Piano Quintet No. 1* (III)

END OF EDITION